Mathematics in the Toy Store

Copyright © 1978, Macdonald-Raintree, Inc.

All rights reserved. No part of this book may be reproduced
or utilized in any form or by any means, electronic or mechanical,
including photocopying, recording, or by any information storage
and retrieval system, without permission in writing from the
Publisher. Inquiries should be addressed to Raintree Childrens Books,
a division of Macdonald-Raintree, Inc., 205 West Highland Avenue,
Milwaukee, Wisconsin 53203.

Library of Congress Number: 77-19155

1 2 3 4 5 6 7 8 9 0 82 81 80 79 78

Printed and bound in the United States of America.

Library of Congress Cataloging in Publication Data

O'Connor, Vincent F.
   Mathematics in the toy store.

   SUMMARY: Color pictures using a toy store setting
relate mathematics to the child's everyday world.
   1. Mathematics — Juvenile literature. [1. Mathematics. 2. Toys — Pictorial Works] I. Ahlberg,
Janet. II. Title. III. Series.
QA40.5.0257   513   77-19155
ISBN 0-8393-0052-2 lib. bdg.

Educational Consultants
Sally Day, Nancye B. Smith, Mary L. Roepke

WILLIAMSBURG
ELEM. SCHOOL

MATHEMATICS
In the Toy Store

ESEA title IU-B
project 57-79-120
2/12/79
PO# 8441

Words by Vincent F. O'Connor

Pictures by Janet Ahlberg

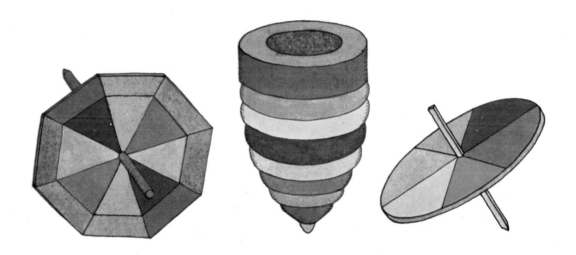

RAINTREE CHILDRENS BOOKS
Milwaukee • Toronto • Melbourne • London

Here is the toy store. The children are
going to buy presents. They will give
the storekeeper their money. He will
give them the change.

These tops have many shapes and colors.
How many tops do you see? Which thing
is not a top? Which top is the biggest?

Look at the sets of toys.
How many dolls do you see?
How many teddy bears are there?

Building blocks have different shapes.
What shapes do you see?
What could you build with blocks?

 =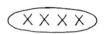

 =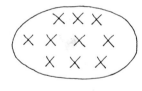

Here are some toy animals in a box.
How many horses? How many *x*'s?
How many horses and sheep?
How many *x*'s?

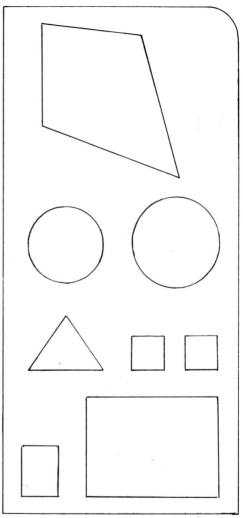

Here are some toys from the store. Look
at their shapes. Now look at the shapes
in the other picture. Do they match
the shapes of the toys?

9

The children are playing with ropes.
How many ropes do you see?
Which straight rope is the longest?
Which is the shortest?

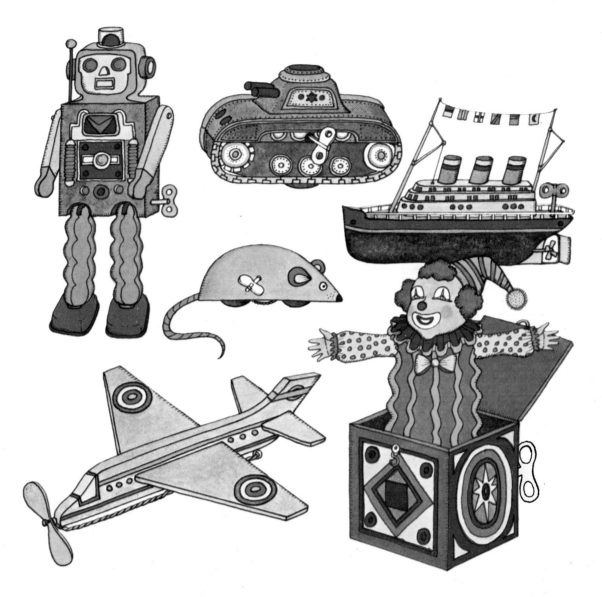

All these toys move. How do you wind
each one up? How many move on
wheels? How many do not?

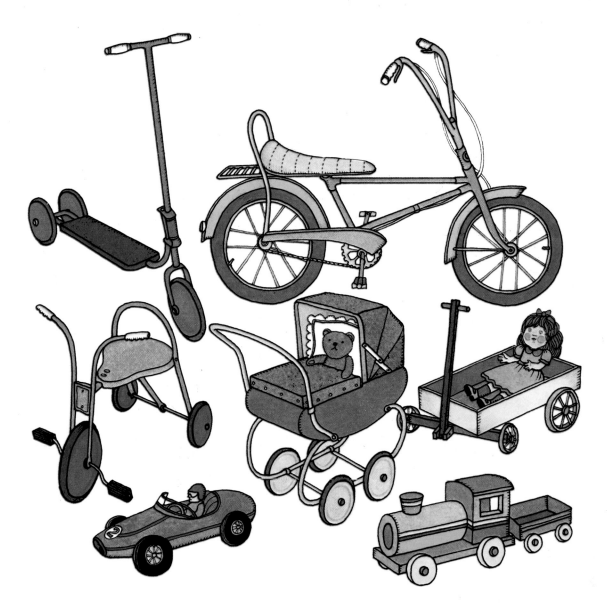

Look at all these toys. Can you name
them? How are all these toys the same?
What else could you put in this set?

Balloons can be different shapes and sizes. Look at the balloons with faces. What happens to the faces when you blow them up?

The children are playing store. They
are using scales to measure things.
The boy finds how many apples
balance the sugar. The girl finds the
mass of the pears.

WILLIAMSBURG
ELEM. SCHOOL

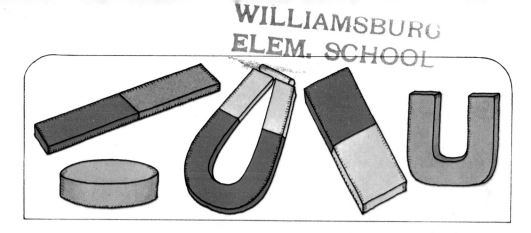

The things at the top are magnets.
Can you guess how they work?
What are the boys doing with magnets?
The girls are playing a fishing game.
What numbers have they caught?

15

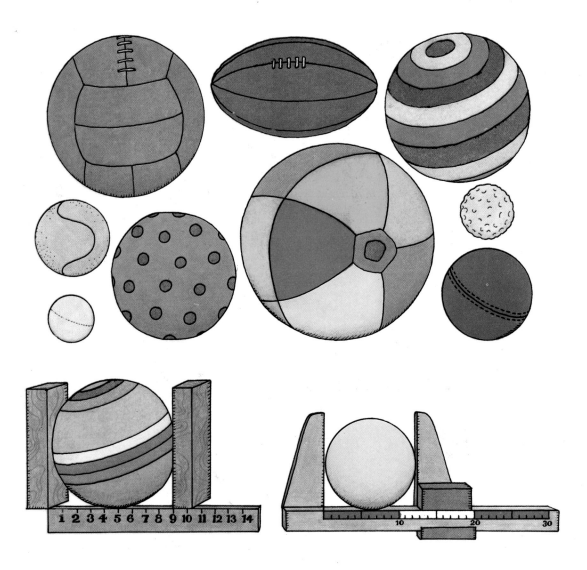

These balls are different sizes. Find the
smallest ball. How can you measure
the size of a ball?

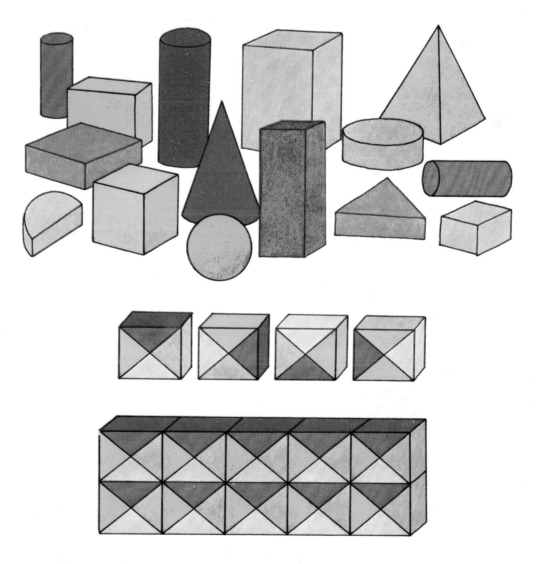

These building blocks have different shapes. Which blocks will roll? Which blocks can slide? Which blocks would you use to build a house?

Here are many kinds of shapes.
The shapes and colors are put together
to make patterns. Which patterns use
many shapes? Which patterns use only
one shape?

The children are wearing dress-up clothes. Different sizes of clothes fit different sizes of people. Do you know the size of your clothes?

Toy rockets can fly across the room.
Real rockets can go far into space.
Which rocket is taller? Which can
go farther?

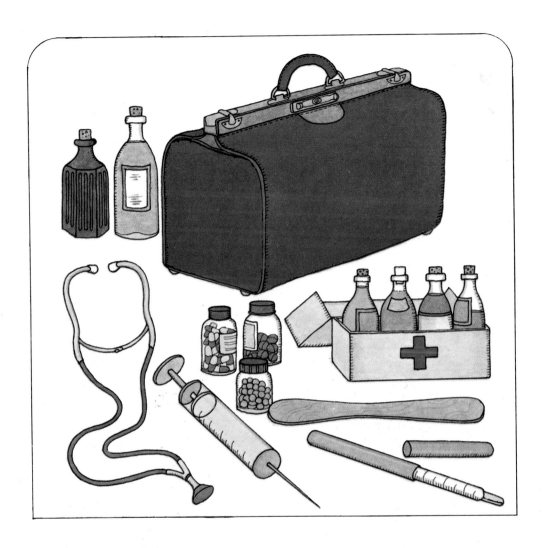

How many things are in this set?
How are these things alike?
Who would use them? Which thing
can carry all of the others?

Here is a set of toys. Which toy is the
tallest? Which is the shortest? Are they
in order of size?

The children are playing with their toys. How many toys have wheels? How many do not have wheels? How many toys are there in all?

Here is a set of racing cars. Count the cars in the set. Which car has the highest number?

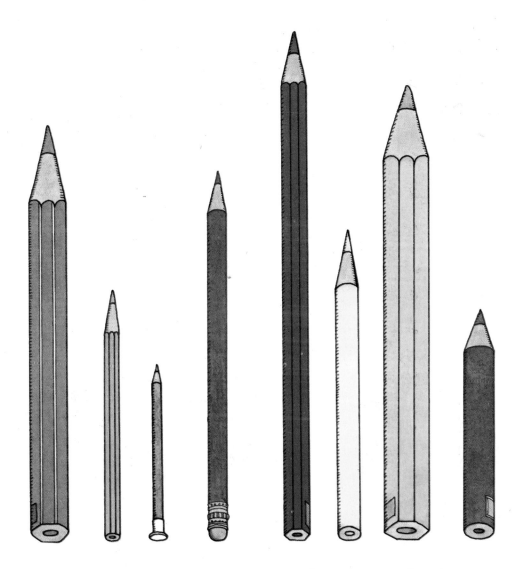

This is a set of pencils. Can you find
the longest one? Which pencil is
the thickest?

Here are some musical instruments.
How many do you see? How many would
you blow? How many would you shake?

What shape is the toy lifting?
Where else do you see that shape?
What shapes do you see in the boxes?
What could you make with them?

Look at the page numbers. Which numbers are even? Which numbers are odd? How many pages in this book have even numbers?

Here are three toy mills. The water mill
has a round wheel. Moving water turns
this wheel. What makes the other
mills turn?

ABOUT THE AUTHOR

VINCENT F. O'CONNOR was granted his B.A. from
the College of St. Thomas and his M.S. from the
University of Notre Dame. He has been a mathematics
teacher, supervisor, and curriculum specialist for
13 years. He had an active role in field testing
a mathematics program for kindergarten through sixth
grade in connection with the National Science Foundation
and the University of Wisconsin. Mr. O'Connor is
currently Mathematics Curriculum Specialist for the
Milwaukee Public Schools. He is also the president
of the Wisconsin Mathematics Council. Mr. O'Connor is a
frequent speaker and workshop leader at meetings of
the National Council of Teachers of Mathematics and
at state and local mathematics conferences.